W.E.B. DU BOIS

and Racial Relations

by Seamus Cavan

GATEWAY CIVIL RIGHTS
THE MILLBROOK PRESS
BROOKFIELD, CONNECTICUT

Published by The Millbrook Press
2 Old New Milford Road, Brookfield, Connecticut 06804

Library of Congress Cataloging-in-Publication Data
Cavan, Seamus.
W.E.B. Du Bois and racial relations / by Seamus Cavan.
p.   cm.—(Gateway civil rights)
Includes bibliographical references and index.
Summary: Examines the life of the black scholar and leader, with
an emphasis on his work for racial equality in the United States.
ISBN 1-56294-288-3 (lib. bdg.)
1. Du Bois, W.E.B. (William Edward Burghardt), 1868–1963—
Juvenile literature.   2. Afro-Americans—Biography—Juvenile
literature.   3. Civil rights workers—United States—Biography—
Juvenile literature.   4. National Association for the Advancement
of Colored People—Biography—Juvenile literature.   5. United
States—Race relations—Juvenile literature.   [1. Du Bois, W.E.B.
(William Edward Burghardt), 1868–1963.   2. Civil rights workers.
3. Afro-Americans—Biography.]   I. Title.   II. Series.
E185.97.D73C38   1993
305.896′073′0092—dc20   [B]   92-33015   CIP   AC

THE NEW NEGRO
HAS NO FEAR

A parade sweeps through New York City's Harlem, about 1925.

William Edward Burghardt Du Bois, by Frederick J. Campbell.

When *W.E.B. Du Bois* was growing up in Great Barrington, Massachusetts, in the 1870s, he believed that he lived in a "boy's paradise." The town was quiet and friendly, and he and his mother, Mary Burghardt Du Bois, were very happy there. Mary worked cleaning and cooking in other people's houses, and although she did not make much money, her only child was always well fed and nicely dressed, and he had lots of friends.

"The little family of my mother and myself must often have been near the edge of poverty," W.E.B. Du Bois wrote many years later. "Yet I was not hungry or in lack of suitable clothing and shoes, or made to feel unfortunate."

But Du Bois's happiness in Great Barrington ended when he was still a young schoolboy. When the boys and girls at his school would visit one another at home, they would leave their calling cards. One day Du Bois and some of his friends visited a new girl in town. As they left, the visitors gave the newcomer their calling cards. She accepted all except one. She refused to take a card from Du Bois. He was the only black in the group. This was the first time he experienced racial prejudice, and it changed him.

From that time on, Du Bois knew that his black skin made him an outcast in some places. He became aloof and quiet, and he spent much less time playing games and socializing. Instead, he read—all the books in the Great Barrington library on history, much of its science section, and many of the world's great novels and poems. Although he did not know it yet, he was preparing himself for his future career as the most important black American scholar and leader of the first half of the twentieth century.

The Secret of Life

William Edward Burghardt Du Bois was born in Great Barrington on February 23, 1868. His father, Alfred Du Bois, left his family shortly after William, later known as W.E.B., was born. But the boy and his mother did not miss him very much. Mother and son were unusually close. Many days, when Mary finished work, William would come to meet her, and the two of them would walk home together to their small clapboard house on Church Street, arm in arm.

Although there were only about fifty blacks in Great Barrington, William rarely felt out of place there in his early years, because unlike many parts of the United States at that time, Massachusetts did not allow segregation—the legal separation of whites and blacks. Du Bois remembered romping around the "quiet hills" of the Berkshire Mountains with children of the town, both black and white, and sailing boats on the "golden"

William grew up in a small, peaceful Massachusetts town much like this one. He and his mother were poor, but for the most part they were happy.

Housatonic River. At school he was known as the "teacher's pet" because he was an excellent student. His mother insisted that he study hard and earn good grades. Getting ahead, she said, "was all a matter of ability and hard work." It was a lesson he took to heart. "The secret of life," he later wrote, "lay in excellence, in accomplishment."

Until the incident with the girl and the calling card, William did not know that some people would treat him unfairly because of the color of his skin. Afterward, he worked even harder. He devoted whatever spare time he had to his studies. "I found it difficult and even unnecessary to approach other people," he said, "and my inner life grew the richer."

To earn money to buy all the books he wanted to read, William delivered newspapers and groceries, chopped wood, shoveled coal, and mowed lawns. He became such a good reader and writer that as a teenager he was hired to write articles for the local newspaper. When he graduated from Great Barrington High School in 1884, William was not only the first black to graduate from the school, he was by far the top student in his class. But he was not satisfied; he was determined to attend Harvard University, one of the best colleges in the nation.

The Young Scholar

W.E.B. Du Bois was the kind of student Harvard was proud to educate. He was very bright, well-read, and interested in the issues of the day. Almost everyone who knew him agreed that he was a very special young man. But his mother did not have the money to send him to college, and Harvard did not want to accept him. Although his principal, a teacher, and two minis-

Children pick cotton on a plantation in the post-Civil War South. At Fisk, Du Bois saw that in parts of the country segregation was still the law.

ters raised enough money to pay his way they suggested that he go to Fisk University, a black college in Nashville, Tennessee, instead. Du Bois, who still wanted to go to Harvard, did not want to go to Fisk. In the South, where most black Americans lived, segregation was practiced, and many blacks were desperately poor. Du Bois called it the "land of slaves," and he did not want to go to school there.

Soon he changed his mind. In Great Barrington, he had not had the opportunity to meet many black people, but at Fisk he would be surrounded by them. He had begun to think that he wanted to spend his life doing something to help black Americans. In order to do so, he would have to learn about how most of them lived.

Du Bois studied at Fisk from September 1885 to June 1888. Once again, he was an excellent student and was also editor of

Although Du Bois did not at first want to go to Fisk, he soon changed his mind. He sits here (left) with members of his graduating class.

the campus newspaper. In the summer, he taught at black schools in the countryside, where he was heartbroken by the poverty that he saw. At Fisk, he felt protected and secure. Never before had he been among so many fellow blacks, and the opportunity to make friends with other young people like himself excited him. But the world outside the Fisk campus could still be an unfriendly place, he knew, where segregation was the law, and he tried to avoid white people. He refused to talk to them, and he looked for friendship only among blacks. He had begun to practice what he called "voluntary segregation." If whites were going to discriminate against blacks, then he would have nothing to do with whites.

After earning his bachelor's degree at Fisk, Du Bois tried once again to go to Harvard. By this time, Harvard was opening its doors to blacks, and he was accepted. He was even offered a scholarship. He spent the next four years there and received a bachelor's degree in philosophy and a master's degree in history and political science. At Harvard, as at Fisk, he made friends only with black people.

In 1892, Du Bois went to Germany on a scholarship. German universities were then some of the best in the world in the new field of sociology, which Du Bois wanted to study. Sociology is the scientific study of human society. Du Bois wanted to use his knowledge in this field to help him study the problems of blacks in American society.

Du Bois learned an important lesson in Germany, but not in the classroom. There was no segregation there, and the people he met did not seem to look down on him because he was black. He made many white friends and even fell in love with a white woman. Although he would spend his life working to end the injustices committed by white Americans against black Americans, never again would Du Bois judge people solely by the color of their skin. He would treat others the way he wanted to be treated. He began to look at whites as individuals: "Slowly they became, not white folks, but just folks," he wrote. "I ceased to hate or suspect people simply because they belonged to one race or color."

Murder on Our Doorsteps

When Du Bois returned from Europe in 1894, it was time to find a job. He wanted a position that would prepare him to become "a leader of my people," but he was not choosy. "I was not exacting or hard to please," he wrote. "I just got down on my knees and begged for work, anything and any-where." Finally, he took a job as a professor at Wilberforce University in Ohio, where he taught for two years and finished writing a study on the slave trade in the United States. His study earned him a Ph.D., or doctorate, which is the highest degree a scholar can receive. Du Bois was the first black American to have one.

Du Bois left Wilberforce to take an even better job as an assistant instructor of sociology at the University of Pennsylvania. He was also given the chance to prepare a report on conditions in the Seventh Ward, a poor, mostly black neighborhood in Philadelphia.

Nina with their son, Burghardt, who died in childhood.

In the meantime, Du Bois had met Nina Gomer, who was, in his own words, "a beautiful, dark-eyed slip of a girl." They married on May 12, 1896.

With his new bride, Du Bois moved to the Seventh Ward in 1896. The Seventh Ward was a very rough, very violent section of the city. Many of the people who lived there did not have jobs. Many were addicted to drugs or alcohol. Many lived lives of very little hope. Each time they left their tiny apartment, Du Bois and Nina had to be very careful. "Murder sat on our doorsteps," Du Bois wrote.

But he disagreed with those politicians and other leaders who said that the problems in the Seventh Ward were the result of the inferior character of black Americans. To Du Bois, the problems of poverty could only be solved by a scientific approach that relied on facts, not on stereotypes and prejudice.

Poverty, crime, and hopelessness existed in places like the Seventh Ward, Du Bois said, because black Americans were not given a fair opportunity to make something of themselves. They received an inferior education in segregated schools, which meant they could not expect to get good jobs. Few employers hired black Americans, and few landlords would rent them good apartments or houses.

Every day, Du Bois walked through the Seventh Ward, asking questions. How old are you? How many children do you have? How much education do you have? What do you want out of life? He recorded the results in his report, "The Philadelphia Negro," which was the first sociological study made of a poor black neighborhood in the United States.

This report made Du Bois one of the nation's top black scholars. He accepted a new position as professor of history at Atlanta University in Georgia. There, Du Bois organized a yearly conference of black scholars who met to discuss their research on the problems affecting black Americans. The results of their findings were published. Du Bois's reports were the only scientific studies of black life then being done.

Besides his scientific work, Du Bois also began to speak out about the way blacks were mistreated. He spoke before Congress about the need for better education of blacks. He made forceful arguments against segregation, and he protested against lynchings of black people.

A lynching was the killing of a person by a mob. In the United States, most often white mobs lynched black men. Sometimes the person being lynched had been accused of a crime, but the mob did not wait for a trial to determine innocence or guilt. Sometimes, the person lynched had done nothing wrong at all, other than having been born with black skin. In the 1890s, one black man was lynched in the United States

In Mississippi a mob of white men took the law into their own hands and hung this young black man before he had a proper trial. Du Bois fought hard to end such lynchings.

THE INVISIBLE EMPIRE OF THE KKK

The Ku Klux Klan, also called the KKK, is a group of white people who are against the integration of blacks, Jews, and other minorities. The Klan, which dates from the end of the Civil War in 1865, has a history of violence.

During the 1800s, Klan members threatened, whipped, tortured, and killed many people, particularly blacks in the South and their supporters. Members often burned huge crosses and hid behind long white robes and pointed hoods during their outdoor meetings in the night.

Du Bois fought hard to put an end to groups such as this one, known as the Invisible Empire. But their number kept growing. By the mid-1920s, the KKK had more than two million members. Although only a few thousand people now belong to the Klan, this racist organization has still not disappeared for good.

A 1926 Ku Klux Klan parade in front of the Capitol.

about every three days. The main purpose of these lynchings was to make other blacks too afraid to speak out for equal rights or against segregation. The threat of lynching was used to force blacks to move off land that whites wanted.

To speak out against such practices took a great deal of courage, but Du Bois was not afraid. He believed that those blacks who had been fortunate enough, like himself, to receive a good education and find good jobs should help improve conditions for other blacks. Already Du Bois had done much, but his work was just beginning.

The Souls of Black Folk

In 1903, Du Bois published his well-known book, *The Souls of Black Folk,* a collection of his most important articles. The theme of the fourteen essays was the unique identity of black Americans. According to Du Bois, racism made blacks look at themselves through the eyes of others because blacks were always aware of how they appeared to whites. So, black people possessed two personalities, two souls, two identities. One was their personality as they knew themselves to be. The other was the personality they had to present to the white world. A black American always "feels his twoness," Du Bois wrote. "Two souls, two thoughts, two unreconciled strivings."

But the part of Du Bois's book that received the most attention was his criticism of Booker T. Washington, the most famous black leader in the country. Washington believed that blacks would never be treated fairly in American society until they escaped from poverty. More importantly, he believed that blacks should not be concerned with ending segregation or obtaining the right to vote until they had improved themselves economically. Once blacks had raised themselves from poverty, whites would be more likely to give them equal rights.

Du Bois could not agree with Washington on this point. He believed that blacks should not have to wait until whites decided they deserved equal rights. Blacks were citizens of the United States, he argued, no matter how poor they were, and they were entitled to the same rights as all other Americans. Du Bois did not believe that blacks should have to ''earn'' the same rights that white Americans automatically enjoyed.

The disagreement between the two leaders became bitter. Du Bois was sure that Washington's policies were harmful to blacks. He became especially angry when Washington said that blacks should settle for low-paying jobs rather than attempt to go to college. Finally, Washington said that blacks should accept segregation if whites would allow them to have their own institutions and organizations.

This was more than Du Bois could stand. Blacks did not have to be allowed things by whites, he argued. They should

BOOKER T. WASHINGTON

Booker Taliaferro Washington was born in 1856, only twelve years before W.E.B. Du Bois. The two men were both powerful black leaders and educators. But they held opposing views about racial problems in the United States.

Washington was born into slavery in Virginia. After the slaves were freed in 1865, he worked in the coal mines of West Virginia. He then went to the Hampton Institute, a school that taught its black students useful skills in order to get jobs on farms and in factories.

Washington founded the Tuskegee Institute, a vocational school for blacks, in 1881. He believed in the importance of a practical, rather than a college, education. If blacks learned skills, worked hard, and earned enough money to buy land, he said, they would be given civil and political rights. Washington explained his ideas in a famous book called *Up from Slavery*.

His early life was very different from that of Du Bois. Washington's ideas about the place of blacks in society reflect this difference.

be treated the same as whites simply because they, too, were Americans. He decided to start his own organization for black equality. Word went out that a meeting was to be held in June 1905 at Niagara Falls. What was needed now, Du Bois said, was "organized determination and aggressive action on the part of men who believe in black freedom and growth." No man was more organized and determined than W.E.B. Du Bois himself.

Peace Will Be My Applause

A number of leading black scholars and leaders went to the meeting Du Bois organized at Niagara Falls. There, the Niagara Movement was born. Its members believed in the "abolition [end] of all caste distinctions based simply on race or color" and "the principle of human brotherhood." Du Bois edited the Niagara Movement's journal. He was also still a professor at Atlanta University, and continued to write books and articles.

The leaders of the Niagara Movement pose in front of the Falls. Du Bois is second from the right in the second row.

In 1909, a group of blacks and whites who cared very much about civil rights founded a new organization. At first, it was called the National Negro Committee. Its name was soon changed to the National Association for the Advancement of Colored People (NAACP). The NAACP would become the most successful civil rights organization in American history.

Du Bois was named the organization's director of publications and research. He resigned from his post at Atlanta University and moved to New York City, where he edited the NAACP journal, *Crisis.* The purpose of *Crisis,* Du Bois wrote, was to "record important happenings and movements in the world which bear on the great problem of interracial relations."

Du Bois in the Crisis *office.*

For the next twenty-four years, Du Bois spent most of his time and energy working on *Crisis*. It soon became the most important and popular magazine of its kind in America. His articles made Du Bois the most important black leader in America, even though many of his positions were unpopular. At one point, for example, he was criticized for writing that blacks should arm themselves in order to resist lynchings and unprovoked attacks. And some of the white leaders of the NAACP were upset that Du Bois listed all the lynchings that took place in the United States. In the 1930s, when the Great Depression left millions of Americans poor and out of work, Du Bois called for ''voluntary segregation.'' Blacks, he said, should make segregation work for them by pooling their money, skills, and goods and backing only black businesses.

Du Bois's support for voluntary segregation angered the leadership of the NAACP, and in 1934 he was made to resign as editor of *Crisis*. It was one of the saddest moments in his long and distinguished career. He said it was like "giving up a child."

Even though he was now sixty-six years old, Du Bois was not ready to retire from the struggle for black equality. He returned to Atlanta University and resumed his career as an educator. He also continued to write and publish books, including *Black Reconstruction,* his famous study of the role played by blacks in the South in the years following the Civil War.

At times, Du Bois felt blacks would never achieve equality. Segregation remained the law in most of America through the 1940s, and even those blacks who fought to defend the United States in World War II were discriminated against when they returned. "The colored people of America are coming to face the fact quite simply that most white Americans do not like them," a tired and sad Du Bois wrote.

He began to travel to other countries to see if there were places where people lived together in greater peace than they did in the United States. In the 1950s, he visited the Soviet Union and China, but his trips got him in trouble with the U.S. government, which did not like its citizens visiting communist countries. But Du Bois believed that Americans could learn something from countries "where people are not taught and encouraged to despise and look down on some class, group, or race."

COLORED
WAITING ROOM
INTRASTATE PASSENGERS →

PULLMAN PASSENGERS
CHECK WITH PULLMAN
CONDUCTOR AT RECEIVING
TABLE BEFORE GOING TO
TRAINS 4-11 & 36
CARS A-4 54-47 & S-58

*Young black men who had fought
for their country in World War II
were still treated like inferior
citizens when they came home.*

The president of Lincoln University presents awards
to Mary McLeod Bethune, a prominent educator, and W.E.B.
Du Bois for their leadership in the fight for equal rights.

In 1954, the Supreme Court of the United States ruled that segregation in public schools was illegal. The question of segregation had been brought before the Supreme Court by the NAACP, and Du Bois felt very proud of the organization he had helped to create. The Supreme Court's ruling was a great victory for black Americans, but "we are not free yet," Du Bois said. Blacks were still the poorest members of American society and were still discriminated against in many different ways.

And Du Bois, then in his eighties, was still active in the fight against these injustices. He continued to write. In 1957, at the age of eighty-nine, he wrote his second novel. Two years later, he wrote another. W.E.B. Du Bois wrote a total of twenty-one books. There were novels, biographies, long historical studies, and shorter essays. All concerned the brave fight of black Americans to gain their equal rights.

In 1961, at the age of ninety-three, Du Bois moved to the newly independent African nation of Ghana. Ghana's first president, Kwame Nkrumah, had invited Du Bois to come live there and prepare an encyclopedia of black African history. Du Bois welcomed the chance to spend his last years in a country where blacks controlled political power and their own future. To black Africans, Du Bois's work for

Du Bois continued his work in Ghana, where he moved at the age of ninety-three.

black freedom and equality had made him one of the greatest men of his time. They said that his example had inspired them to fight for freedom in their own countries. Many of Africa's most important writers and leaders came to visit him in his new home in Accra, the capital of Ghana. They called him the "father of Africa" and "Ghana's first citizen."

Du Bois died in Accra on August 27, 1963. He was ninety-five years old, and every one of those years had been filled with excellence and achievement. Before he died, he wrote a last message to be read aloud at his funeral. He urged people never to stop working to make the world a fairer place to live. "One thing alone, I ask you," his message read. "As you live, believe in life." Someday, all human beings will learn how to live together in peace, he wrote, "and that peace will be my applause."

Facing page:
Du Bois spoke at the 1949 World
Peace Conference in Paris, France.
He was sad that Americans did
not live in peace together.

IMPORTANT EVENTS IN THE LIFE OF W.E.B. DU BOIS

1868   William Edward Burghardt (W.E.B.) Du Bois is born on February 23 in Great Barrington, Massachusetts.

1888   Du Bois graduates from Fisk University in Nashville.

1892   Du Bois graduates from Harvard University with degrees in philosophy and history and political science.

1896   Du Bois receives a doctorate in history from Harvard. He marries Nina Gomer.

1897   Du Bois begins teaching history at Atlanta University, Georgia.

1899   Du Bois publishes "The Philadelphia Negro," his landmark sociological study of a black neighborhood.

1903   Du Bois publishes *The Souls of Black Folk.*

1909   Du Bois helps to found the NAACP. He becomes the editor of *Crisis* magazine.

1961   Du Bois moves to the country of Ghana in Africa.

1963   On August 27, W.E.B. Du Bois dies in Accra, Ghana.

FIND OUT MORE
ABOUT W.E.B. DU BOIS
AND HIS TIMES

Booker T. Washington by Jan Gleiter and Kathleen Thompson (Milwaukee: Raintree, 1987).

The Civil Rights Movement in America from 1865 to the Present by Patricia and Fredrick McKissack (Chicago: Childrens Press, 1987).

W.E.B. Du Bois by Patricia and Fredrick McKissack (New York: Franklin Watts, 1990).

W.E.B. Du Bois by Mark Stafford (New York: Chelsea House Publishers, 1989).

W.E.B. Du Bois: A Biography by Virginia Hamilton (New York: HarperCollins Children's Books, 1987).

INDEX